YES....I CAN

THE POWER OF AFFIRMATION

DR. PARTHA GOSWAMI

Dedicated To

All Positive Souls

Contents

Positive Affirmation By Partha Goswami   vii

Foreword   ix

Preface   xi

Acknowledgements   xiii

Prologue   xv

Yes...I Can

Powerful Mantra

1. Aum (ॐ)   5

2. Shiva Mantra   6

3. Gayatri Mantra   7

4. Maha Mrityunjaya Mantra   8

5. What Are Mantras   9

6. How Do Mantras Work?   10

7. Spiritual Affirmation   11

Crown Chakras

8. Crown Chakra Affirmations   15

9. Mantras & Affirmations   17

10. Root Chakra   18

11. Sacral Chakra   19

12. Solar Plexus Chakra   20

13. Heart Chakra   21

14. Throat Chakra   22

15. Third Eye Chakra   23

16. Crown Chakra   25

Positive Affirmations

17. Positive Affirmations   29

18. What Is Affirmation ?   31

19. Example   33

Contents

20. Benefits Of Affirmations — 35

21. How To Use — 38

22. How To Write — 39

23. Making Effective Affirmation — 40

24. Make A Habit — 41

25. Practice Affirmation — 43

26. Creating Affirmations — 44

Quotes

27. Special Quote — 47

28. Swami Vivekananda — 48

29. Famous Quotes — 56

How To Start

30. Using Positive Affirmations — 63

Books By Author — 67

POSITIVE AFFIRMATION BY PARTHA GOSWAMI

A Wing Of Vybez Systems Frameworks Pvt. Ltd.

Edited By : Hrit Hrishant

Graphics : Collected

Information : Collected

Price : Rs. 249.00

~

Vybez Systems Frameworks Pvt. Ltd.
Shibpur, Howrah, West Bengal - 711102
Email : vfstech.info@gmail.com
Visit Us : www.vfstech.info

Foreword

"If you fail, never give up because

F.A.I.L means First Attempt In Learning.

End is not the end, if fact

E.N.D. means Effort Never Dies.

If you get No as an answer, remember

N.O. means Next Opportunity."

--- Dr. A P J Abdul Kalam

Preface

I just try to discuss with all youngers the power of Affirmation. This book is for all. Positive affirmations are a great way to give yourself a boost of confidence and to help you start your day on the right foot. While it may seem like a silly concept, affirmations can be powerful tools for shifting your mindset and attitude.

In this Book, I will discuss the power of positive affirmations, why they work, and how to incorporate them into your daily life. In the world of personal development, positive affirmations are becoming increasingly recognized for the positive impact they can have on a person's life. They can be used to reinforce positive beliefs, foster a sense of self-worth, and motivate you to take action towards achieving your goals. Ultimately, positive affirmations will help you become the best version of yourself and can be used as a tool to make positive changes in your life.

Dr. Partha Goswami
gp1980.com@gmail.com

Acknowledgements

To everyone at the Vybez Team who enables me to be the CEO of a company that I'm honored to be a part of, thank you for letting me serve, for being a part of our amazing company, and for showing up every day and helping more authors turn their ideas into stories.

Without the experiences and support from my peers and team at Vybez, this book would not exist. You have given me the opportunity to lead a great group of individuals—to be a leader of great leaders is a blessed place to be. Thank you to All.

Prologue

A book about the power of positive affirmations for all aspects of life, from building self-confidence and overcoming depression to gaining confidence and achieving spiritual enlightenment.

Yes...I Can

Sound of The Universe

Powerful Mantra

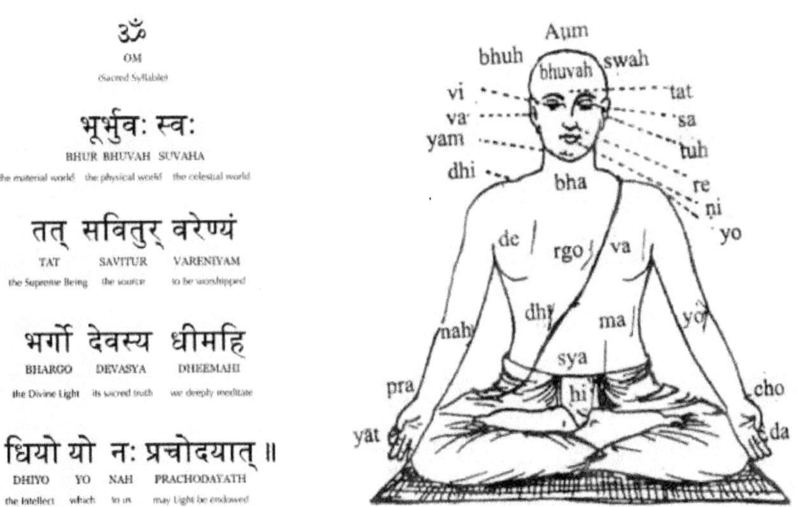

The Power of Mantras

I
Aum (ॐ)

AUM

Aum (OM) is known to be the sound of the universe. It can bring lots of benefits to you by getting your being to harmony with nature and the universe. Universal sound. First, the actual vibration, representing birth, death and the process of rebirth.

It is said that just singing OM, 3 times, can reduce your heart rate and make you feel 20% calm in just a few seconds. Singing the OM of sound brings us to harmonic resonance and the universe – this is the truth of science! OM is said to be performing at 432 Hertz, which is the Universe's natural musical voice.

Reducing your frequency to match the Atmosphere silences mood swings, allowing you to practice yoga with sound. OM is an unusual way to start and end a practice of yoga or meditation.

II
Shiva Mantra

Aum Namah Shivaya (ॐ नमः शिवाय)

Shiva is a primary deity in Hinduism. A male force, he is the creator and the destroyer. His mantra is perfect for bringing your mind to order with all the forces of the universe.

It means "I bow down to Shiva," which is your true inner self, the divine consciousness that dwells within each of us.
Om Namah Shivaya is a very powerful mantra and is one of the most famous Hindu mantras. This mantra is believed to aid in the destruction of dignity and the rebirth of the soul.

Aum Namah Shivaya is a 5-syllable mantra. When you chant this Aum Namah Shivaya, you call on Shiva to destroy, to dissolve your own self to become a new you.

III
Gayatri Mantra

Gayatri Mantra

"Om bhūr bhuvaḥ svaḥ
tát savitúr váreṇ(i)yaṃ
bhárgo devásya dhīmahi
dhíyo yó naḥ prachodayat"

The Gayatri mantra is highly revered in every word, found in the RigVeda. Goddess Gayatri is also called "Veda-Mata" or Mother Vedas – Rig, Yajur, Saam, and Atharva – because they are the very foundation of the Vedas. Basically, the truth behind the knowledgeable universe and the known universe.

The Gayatri mantra is composed of a meter consisting of 24 syllables – usually arranged in a triplet of eight words each. Therefore, this meter (tripadhi) is also known as the Gayatri Meter or "Gayatri Chhanda."

IV
Maha Mrityunjaya Mantra

Mahamrityunjaya Mantra

Om tryambakam yajaamahe
sugandhim pushthivardhanam;
Urvaarukamiva bandhanaan
Mrityormuksheeya maamritaat.

Maha Mrityunjaya mantra has been proved to be healing and life-saving since ages in Hinduism. This mantra should be chanted with Yagya or Hawan which purifies your inner self and air of all the unwanted germs and energies. It is called the Maha Mrityunjaya mantra, the Great Death-Conquering mantra. Aum Haum Juum Sah. Aum Bhuurbhuvah Svah. Aum Tryambakam Yajaamahe, Sugandhim Pushtivardhanam Urvaarukamiva bandhanaan, Mrityurmokshiya Maamrataat. Aum Svah Bhuvah Bhuuh Aum Sah Juum Haum Aum. Maha Mrityunjaya mantra has been proved to be healing and life-saving since ages in Hinduism. This mantra should be chanted with Yagya or Hawan which purifies your inner self and air of all the unwanted germs and energies. It is called the Maha Mrityunjaya mantra, the Great Death-Conquering mantra.

V
What Are Mantras

What Are Mantras

The word mantra in the Sanskrit language means "the thought that liberates and protects". The root of the word "man" means to think, and "tra" means to protect or to liberate.

Mantras are sacred sounds created by ancient Indian sages and yogis. These sages and yogis managed to become one with nature and the environment around them. They heard sounds and vibrations of things surround them and expressed these sounds as mantras.

VI
How do Mantras work?

How do Mantras work?

Mantras will work if you chant them regularly. It doesn't matter if you chant them out loud or in silence. Before you start chanting, you should set your intention.

Mantras are tools that can help you feel alive and reach an inner state of contentment. The mantras' power lies in the vibration produced by the utterance of the mantra. There are countless mantras, so you need to choose the one that best fits your intention.

Some mantras have a melodic sound and a beautiful meaning. But the meaning of the mantra is not essential. The vibration of the mantra will harmonise you with the universe.

The vibration of a mantra will help you recognise your divinity. You will feel at ease with life as you progress in mantra chanting.

The sound of a mantra carries a specific power. You can use that power to align your vibration with the mantra. After chanting for three months, you will start seeing the benefits of chanting mantras. A mantra will work for the intention you set. For mantras, the meaning of the word is not essential, unlike affirmations.

VII
Spiritual Affirmation

Spiritual Affirmation

A spiritual affirmation is *usually a sentence or phrase that you repeat regularly to make a formal declaration to yourself and the universe ...*

MANTRAS & AFFIRMATIONS

Most people use mantras and affirmations interchangeably. However, they are not the same.

Mantras and affirmations are different. Mantras are sounds that carry a vibration to get you in harmony with the universe. Affirmations are positive statements to help you reprogram your mind. Both of them can help you improve yourself, accept yourself, and achieve your goals.

Crown Chakras

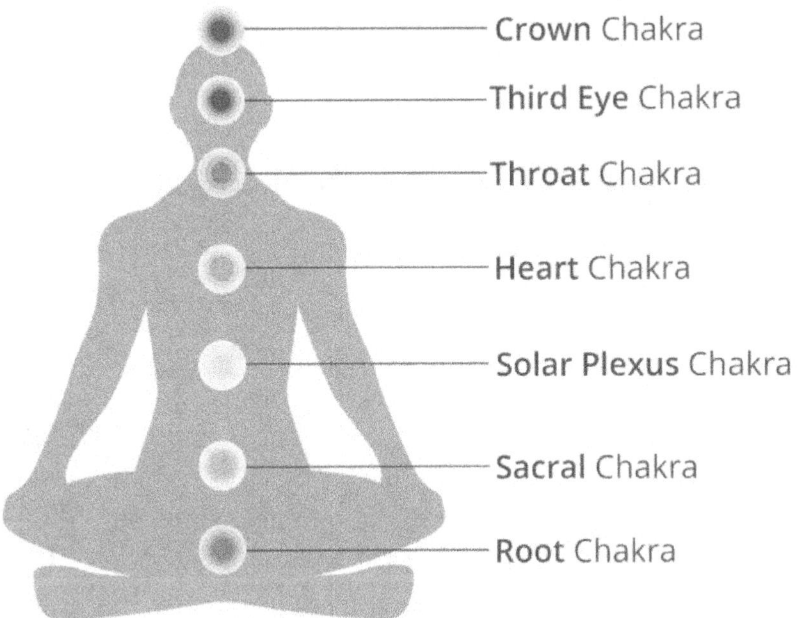

The Crown Chakra

VIII
Crown Chakra Affirmations

Crown Chakra Affirmations for Spiritual Awakening

Invoke your spiritual awakening and awareness of life's purpose with crown chakra affirmations.

In Sanskrit, the word "chakra" means "disk" or "wheel" and refers to the energy centers in the body. These wheels or disks of spinning energy each relate to certain nerve bundles and major organs.

There are 7 chakras (root, sacral, solar plexus, heart, throat, third eye, and crown). Today we will focus on **Crown Chakra (also called Sahasrara) Affirmations.**

The **Crown Chakra** is located at the top of the head. It is highly connected to spirituality. Related to our connection with the supreme Self. A balanced crown chakra leads to spiritual enlightenment and the awareness of life's purpose.

I am fully aware & awake
I am always divinely & lovingly guided.
I honor the Divine with me.
I am a spiritual being in a Human body.
I am pure, beautiful, radiant light.
I am deeply and unconditionally loved by the Universe.
I surrender to the loving will of the Universe.

I release doubt and welcome faith.
I can achieve anything.

IX
Mantras & Affirmations

Seven Chakras

MANTRAS AND AFFIRMATIONS FOR EACH CHAKRA

Here are some Chakra-specific *mantras* and *affirmations* that you can use daily - during your practice, on- or off- the mat.

X

Root Chakra

Muladhara Chakra (Root Chakra)

Muladhara chakra represents our foundation. When outbalanced, an individual feels ungrounded, unstable, insecure, fearful, and frustrated with a lack of ambition & purpose. When the root chakra is balanced, these negative emotions are replaced by positive emotions, making you feel stable, confident, balanced, energetic, independent, and strong.

Function: Survival, Financial Independence, Stability, Security, Self-confidence

Beej Mantra: 'Lam'

Color: Red

Element: Earth

Stone: Hematite

Yoga posture for Balancing: Virabhadrasana (Warrior Pose), Vrkshasana (Tree Pose), Tadasana (Mountain Pose), Ardha Setu Bandhasana (Half Bridge Pose), Shavasana (Corpse Pose)

Age it develops: 1-7 years

Affirmations : I am safe and secure. I am healthy and strong. Life is good.

XI
Sacral Chakra

Swadishthana Chakra (Sacral Chakra)

This Chakra helps us understand the way we relate to our & others' emotions. The sacral chakra also controls sexual energy and creativity.

An individual with a blocked Sacral chakra feels angry, discontented, and emotionally explosive. There's a sense of lack of energy and creativity, feels manipulative, or obsessed with sexual thoughts. When this chakra is balanced, it makes you more positive, happy, vibrant, compassionate, intuitive, and satisfied.

Location: Lower abdomen (2-4 fingers below the navel)

Function: Desire and procreation, sexuality, emotions, pleasure, creativity

Beej Mantra: 'Vam'

Color: Orange

Element: Water

Stone: Tiger's Eye, amber, topaz, opal

Yoga posture: Kakasana (Crow Pose), Trikonasana (Triangle Pose), Baddha Konasana (Bound Angle Pose)

Age it develops: 8-14 years old

Affirmations I enjoy my life fully. I am passionate and creative. I am in control of my own sexuality.

XII
Solar Plexus Chakra

Manipura Chakra (Solar Plexus Chakra)

his Chakra relates to an individual's ability to be confident, in control of life, have a sense of belonging, and define self-esteem. Imagine a situation when you had butterflies in the stomach, that was your Manipura Chakra at work. When the Solar Plexus chakra is blocked, one feels extreme self-doubt and shame. By balancing this chakra, we feel free to express our true selves, we are more energetic, confident, productive, and focussed.

Location: Upper abdomen at the solar plexus, between the bottom of the rib cage and navel

Function: Self-esteem, self-confidence, life awareness, action, power, strength, will, and pleasure

Beej Mantra: 'Ram'

Color: Yellow

Element: Fire

Stones: Yellow stones (Amber, Calcite, Citrine, Quartz, and Topaz)

Yoga posture: Paschimottanasana (Classical Forward Bend), Bhujangasana (Classical Cobra Pose), and Dhanurasana (Bow Pose).

Age it develops: 15-21 years old

Affirmations There are no failures. I learn from everything I do. I am confident and powerful. I release judgment.

XIII

Heart Chakra

Anahata Chakra (Heart Chakra)

This chakra is the bridge between the lower chakras (accredited with materialism) and the upper chakras (associated with spirituality). Anahata Chakra is the seat of balance and if unbalanced an individual may feel emotional issues like anger, lack of trust, anxiety, jealousy, moodiness, and fear. When balanced a person begins to feel more compassionate, caring, optimistic, friendly, and motivated.

Location: On the cardiac plexus (Heart)

Function: Love, compassion, wisdom, trust, forgiveness, generosity, openness to others

Beej Mantra: 'Yam'

Color: Green or pink

Element: Air

Stone: Rose Quartz

Yoga pose: Ardha Setubandhasana (Half Bridge Pose), Ushtrasana (Camel Pose), and Matsyasana (Fish Pose).

Age it develops: 21-28 years old

Affirmations : I truly love and approve of myself. I forgive myself and let go. I am grateful.

XIV
Throat Chakra

Vishuddha Chakra (Throat Chakra)

The Vishuddha Chakra provides a voice to the Anahata chakra and maintains our ability to communicate our power. Blocking of the throat chakra is experienced as timidity, quietness, and the inability to express our thoughts. When the balance is restored in Throat Chakra, it allows us to express ourselves clearly; it enables positive self-expression, constructive communication, creativity, and a sense of satisfaction.

Location: Base of the throat, coinciding with the thyroid gland

Function: Communication, self-expression, and truth

Beej Mantra: 'Ham'

Color: Light Blue and Turquoise

Element: Sound and Music

Stone: All blue stones Aquamarine, chalcedon, sodalite, lapis lazuli

Yoga posture: Sarvangasana (Shoulderstand), Halasana (Plough Pose), and Matsyasana (Fish Pose)

Age it develops: 29-35 years old

Affirmations It is safe to express my feelings. I am heard. I communicate with clarity and positivity.

XV
Third Eye Chakra

Ajna Chakra (Third Eye Chakra)

Ajna chakra aka Third Eye Chakra, is also used as a focal point to develop more concentration and awareness during asana practice. Moving up the body, we're moving closer to togetherness with the divine. They say meditating upon Ajna chakra destroys the past lives karmas and ushers liberation and intuitive knowledge.

Its attributes are intelligence, insight, self-knowledge, and intuition. If imbalanced, it makes you feel non-assertive and afraid of success; also, it can make you more egoistical and can cause physical problems like headaches, eye strain, seizures, and spinal dysfunctions. When Ajna chakra is balanced and active, an individual feels more confident and vibrant (spiritually and emotionally).

Location: Between the eyebrows (third eye) in the middle of the forehead

Function: Intuition, imagination, foresight, liberation, intellect, clairvoyance,

Beej Mantra: 'Om', 'Aum'

Color: purple or indigo

Element: Light

Stones: Amethyst, sapphire, fluorite, labradorite, opal, moldavite, zircon

Yoga pose: Shirshasana (Headstand). Balasana (Child's Pose)

Age it develops: 36-42 years old

Affirmations I trust my intuition. I am open to new ideas, people, and situations. I see and understand the big picture.

XVI
Crown Chakra

Sahastrara Chakra (Crown Chakra)

The Sahastrara Chakra is the highest Chakra in the human body and it is located at the crown of the head. The seventh chakra is the center of spirituality, dynamic thought, energy, wisdom, and cosmic consciousness. One undergoes destructive feelings and experiences constant frustration and melancholy if the Sahastrara chakra gets blocked or is imbalanced.

Location: Above the head

Function: Spirituality, enlightenment, universal or pure awareness

Beej Mantra: 'Om'

Color: Deep purple, White

Element: Divine Consciousness

Stones: Hyaline quartz, diamond

Yoga Posture: Shirshasana (Headstand)

Age it develops: 43-49 years old

Affirmations I am peace and harmony. I am connected, protected and supported by the Universe. I know my purpose.

Positive Affirmations

Daily Affirmations:

I am worthy

I am confident

I am successful

I am magnetic

I am energized

I am powerful

It's already mine

The Positive Affirmation

XVII
Positive Affirmations

What Is Affirmation ?

Affirmations in New Thought and New Age terminology refer primarily to the practice of positive thinking and self-empowerment—fostering a belief that "a positive mental attitude supported by affirmations will achieve success in anything.

~

~

New-Age affirmations come in different forms:

- **Spiritual Talks**
- **Lectures**
- **Classes**
- **Affirmative Images,**
- **Affirmative Words**
- **Affirmative Videos**
- **Mantra Chants**

~

~

What Are Positive Affirmations?

Positive affirmations are made up of phrases that you can say aloud to yourself or in your head. You can also write them down and make sure they're always visible. Positive affirmations are meant to help build you up and improve your confidence, even when things are difficult.

Example of Positive Affirmations

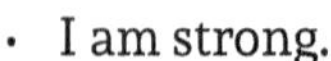

- I am strong.

- I am confident.

- I trust myself.

- I am safe.

- I love myself.

- I believe in myself.

- My possibilities are endless.

- My life is a gift.

- I am strong in my mind, body, and spirit.

- I care for myself.

- I am always learning.

- I Can Do It.

- I have faith in my abilities.

XVIII
What Is Affirmation ?

What Is Affirmation ?

Affirmations in New Thought and New Age terminology refer primarily to the practice of positive thinking and self-empowerment—fostering a belief that "a positive mental attitude supported by affirmations will achieve success in anything.

New-Age affirmations come in different forms:

- **Spiritual Talks**
- **Lectures**
- **Classes**
- **Affirmative Images,**
- **Affirmative Words**
- **Affirmative Videos**
- **Mantra Chants**

What Are Positive Affirmations?

Positive affirmations are made up of phrases that you can say aloud to yourself or in your head. You can also write them down and make sure they're always visible. Positive affirmations are meant to help build you up and improve your confidence, even when things are difficult.

XIX
Example

Example of Positive Affirmations

- I am strong.

- I am confident.

- I trust myself.

- I am safe.

- I love myself.

- I believe in myself.

- My possibilities are endless.

- My life is a gift.

- I am strong in my mind, body, and spirit.

- I care for myself.

- I am always learning.

- I Can Do It.

- I have faith in my abilities.

XX
Benefits of Affirmations

Benefits of Positive Affirmations

- **Decrease Heath-Deteriorating Stress**

"A single word has the power to influence the expression of genes that regulate physical and emotional stress." - **Dr. Andrew Newberg, Neuro Scientist.**

According to a study, there is even a stronger link between stressful life events and mental illnesses.

- **Contro Sef-Sabotaging Thoughts And Speech**

Believing this inner dialogue may leave you feeling sad, depressed, unworthy, and undeserving.

According to an article published by Psych Central, Self-Sabotage : Why You Hold Yourself Back, timely affirmations empower you to shift the internal narrative. Furthermore, by engaging in more positive self-talk, *"...you can begin to stop self-sabotaging and work towards the life you deserve."*

- **Reduce Anxiety**

These habits have a way of making us feel anxious and panicky. In fact, chronic, excessive worrying is a symptom of anxiety disorder.

- **Improve Mood**

They work the same way negative self-talk does. The difference, though, is the many benefits of affirmations on your overall quality of life.

- **Promote Positive Coping**

There is well-established evidence that chronic substance use can cause or worsen mental illness.

- **Enhance Sef-Esteem**

According to The National Alliance on Mental Illness (NAMI), low self-esteem is linked to mental health issues and a poor quality of life.

- **Improve Probem-Solving Under Stress**

A study confirms that people can boost their problem-solving abilities under pressure through Self-Affirmation During the study, chronically stressed participants performed just as well under pressure as participants who had lower stress levels.

- **Can Hep You Find Love**

You can literally attract love into your life by believing that love exists and you're deserving of it. The idea is grounded in a philosophy known as the **Law of Attraction.**

- **May Change Outcomes**

Affirming that the outcome will be different than you earlier anticipated provides motivation to act in ways that lead to pleasant results. According to Amy Morin, Licensed Clinical Social Worker and Editor-in-Chief of VeryWellMind, *"When that frame [point-of-view] is shifted, the meaning changes and thinking and behavior often change along with it."*

- **Improves Your Overal Wellbeing**

You can sleep better, feel more relaxed and be increasingly motivated to exercise.

- **Makes You More Physicaly Active**

That's because repeating your mantra daily aloud actually alters your brain!

- **Eases Depression**

Positive affirmations can be very helpful to combat depression...They offer the brain cognitive restructuring.

- **Makes You More Optimistic**

In this paper he explains how they help to challenge and defeat negative, self-sabotaging thoughts.

- **Heps You Sleep Better**

If the main reason you're having trouble falling asleep is [that] you keep thinking of the stressors you encounter at work, you might come up with affirmations that help you reframe how you think about those stressors: 'I choose to release my work stress' or 'I can control how my work affects me.'

- **Enhances Academic Performance**

It's this heightened sense of awareness that researchers found made people more receptive to errors, allowing them to identify and correct mistakes.

- **Boosts Your IQ**

You might be surprised to hear that **Self-Affirmation Can Actually Boost Your IQ** by as much as 10 points!

XXI
How to Use

How to Use Positive Affirmations

You can use affirmations in any situation where you'd like to see a positive change take place in your life. These might include times when you want to:

- **Raise your confidence before presentations or important meetings.**
- **Control negative feelings such as frustration, anger, or impatience.**
- **Improve your self-esteem.**
- **Finish projects you've started.**
- **Improve your productivity.**
- **Overcome a bad habit.**

Affirmations may be more effective when you pair them with other positive thinking and goal-setting techniques.

XXII
How to Write

How to Write an Affirmation Statement

Affirmation statements usually target a specific area, behavior or belief that you're struggling with. The following points can help you to write the affirmation statement that best fits your needs.

- **Think about the areas of your life that you'd like to change.**
- **Be sure that your affirmation is credible and achievable.**
- **Turn negatives into positives.**
- **Write your affirmation in the present tense.**
- **Say it with feeling.**

XXIII
Making Effective Affirmation

Making Affirmations more effective

Affirmations are just one self-help tool. Like other strategies, they can offer some measure of relief, but their benefits usually depend on how you use them.

Creating your own can help ensure you're choosing affirmations that will help *you* most. Try the tips below to start developing and using affirmations more effectively.

- **Set them in the present**
- **Avoid stock affirmations**
- **Keep it real**
- **Believe it when you affirm**

XXIV
Make A Habit

Make A Habit With Affirmation

To get the most benefit from affirmations, you'll want to start a regular practice and make it a habit :

- **Start with 3 to 5 minutes at least twice a day.** Try saying affirmations upon waking up and getting into bed, for example.
- **Repeat each affirmation about 10 times.** Listen to yourself saying it, focusing on the words as they leave your mouth. As you say them, believe them to be true.
- **Ask a trusted loved one to help.** Listening to someone else repeat your affirmations may help reinforce your belief in them.
- **Make your routine consistent.** Try not to skip any days. If you meditate, affirmations can be a great addition to your daily practice.
- **Be patient.** It may take some time before you notice any changes, so stick with your practice!

~

~

~

Another Benefit Of A Daily Routine?

Practicing affirmations can activate Trusted Source the reward system in your brain, which can have an impact on the way you experience both emotional and physical pain.

Knowing you have the ability to manage stress and other life difficulties can help boost confidence and self-empowerment, further promoting faith in yourself.

The continued repetition of certain thoughts over time has been proven to change your brain, your cells, and even your genes, which is done via neuroplasticity. Essentially, through positive affirmations, individuals can rewire certain thoughts.

XXV
Practice Affirmation

PRACTICE AFFIRMATIONS DAILY BY CREATING A ROUTINE

~

- Speak your affirmations for five minutes 3-5 times daily.
- Repeat your affirmations while looking in the mirror.
- Focus on one affirmation a week, write it down 10-15 times daily
- Record yourself speaking your affirmations.
- Play this audio when you feel overwhelmed or emotionally drained.

XXVI
Creating Affirmations

Creating Affirmations

- Make them short and easy to remember. (3-6 words are ideal).
- Start your affirmations with "I" or "My."
- Write them in the present tense.
- Use statements that declare you already are or have whatever you desire.
- Ensure your affirmations are reasonable and realistic.
- Create a safe space where you can sit, meditate, and recite your affirmations.
- Recite your positive affirmations daily (daily mantra) until they become new core beliefs.

Quotes

Swami Vivekananda

**'Arise, awake, and stop not till the goal is reached. '–
Swami Vivekananda**

XXVII
Special Quote

Be Positive

Role of Daily Affirmations in Everyone's Life

"Watch your thoughts, they become your words; watch your words, they become your actions; watch your actions, they become your habits; watch your habits, they become your character; watch your character, it becomes your destiny." — **Lao Tzu**

XXVIII
Swami Vivekananda

Swami Vivekananda in Present Life

- "In a conflict between the heart and the brain, follow your heart."

  ~

- "Do not wait for anybody or anything. Do whatever you can, build your hope on none."

  ~

- "You have to grow from the inside out. None can teach you, none can make you spiritual. There is no other teacher but your own soul."

  ~

- "Condemn none: if you can stretch out a helping hand, do so. If you cannot, fold your hands, bless your brothers, and let them go their own way."

  ~

- "Do one thing at a time, and while doing it put your whole soul into it to the exclusion of all else."

~

- "We reap what we sow. We are the makers of our own fate. None else has the blame, none has the praise."

~

- "If I love myself despite my infinite faults, how can I hate anyone at the glimpse of a few faults."

~

- "Who is helping you, don't forget them. Who is loving you, don't hate them. Who is believing you, don't cheat them."

~

- "Learn everything that is good from others but bring it in, and in your own way absorb it; do not become others."

~

- "It is our own mental attitude which makes the world what it is for us. Our thought make things beautiful, our thoughts make things ugly. The whole world is in our own minds. Learn to see things in the proper light."

~

- "Watch people do their most common actions; these are indeed the things that will tell you the real character of a great person."

~

- "The difference between architecture and building is that the former expresses an idea, while the latter is merely a structure built on economical principles. The value of matter depends solely on its capacities of expressing ideas."

~

- "Great work requires great and persistent effort for a long time. ...Character has to be established through a thousand stumbles."

~

- "Ask nothing; want nothing in return. Give what you have to give; it will come back to you, but do not think of that now."

~

- "Neither seek nor avoid, take what comes."

~

- "So long as there is desire or want, it is a sure sign that there is imperfection. A perfect, free being cannot have any desire."

~

- "Purity, patience, and perseverance are the three essentials to success and above all, love."

~

- "When an idea exclusively occupies the mind, it is transformed into an actual physical or mental state."

~

- "The more we come out and do good to others, the more our hearts will be purified, and God will be in them."

~

- "Our duty is to encourage everyone in his struggle to live up to his own highest idea, and strive at the same time to make the ideal as near as possible to the Truth."

~

- "We are what our thoughts have made us; so take care about what you think. Words are secondary. Thoughts live; they travel far."

~

- "We are responsible for what we are, and whatever we wish ourselves to be, we have the power to make ourselves. If what we are now has been the result of our own past actions, it certainly follows that whatever we wish to be in the future can be produced by our present actions; so we have to know how to act."

~

- "Each work has to pass through these stages—ridicule, opposition, and then acceptance. Those who think ahead of their time are sure to be misunderstood."

~

- "Comfort is no test of truth. Truth is often far from being comfortable."

~

- "The fire that warms us can also consume us; it is not the fault of the fire."

~

- "Anything that makes weak – physically, intellectually and spiritually, reject it as poison."

~

- "Take up one idea. Make that one idea your life – think of it, dream of it, live on that idea. Let the brain, muscles, nerves, every part of your body, be full of that idea, and just leave every other idea alone. This is the way to success."

~

- "All power is within you; you can do anything and everything. Believe in that, do not believe that you are weak; do not believe that you are half-crazy lunatics, as most of us do nowadays. You can do anything and everything, without even the guidance of anyone. Stand up and express the divinity within you."

~

- "Never think there is anything impossible for the soul. It is the greatest heresy to think so. If there is sin, this is the only sin; to say that you are weak, or others are weak."

~

- "Believe in yourself and the world will be at your feet."

~

- "Whatever you think that you will be. If you think yourself weak, weak you will be; if you think yourself strong, you will be."

~

- "Books are infinite in number and time is short. The secret of knowledge is to take what is essential. Take that and try to live up to it."

~

- "There is no limit to the power of the human mind. The more concentrated it is, the more power is brought to bear on one point."

~

- "Dare to be free, dare to go as far as your thought leads, and dare to carry that out in your life. "

~

- "You can not believe in God until you believe in yourself."

~

- "All knowledge that the world has ever received comes from the mind; the infinite library of the universe is in our own mind."

~

- "Each work has to pass through these stages: ridicule, opposition, and then acceptance. Those who think ahead of their time are sure to be misunderstood."

~

- "They alone live, who live for others."

~

- "The whole life is a succession of dreams. My ambition is to be a conscious dreamer, that is all."

~

- "Are great things ever done smoothly? Time, patience, and indomitable will must show."

~

- "Don't look back – forward, infinite energy, infinite enthusiasm, infinite daring, and infinite patience – then alone can great deeds be accomplished"

~

- "All the powers in the universe are already ours. It is we who have put our hands before our eyes and cry that it is dark."

~

- "Are you unselfish? That is the question. If you are, you will be perfect without reading a single religious book, without going into a single church or temple."

~

- "The greatest religion is to be true to your own nature. Have faith in yourselves."

~

- "I, for one, thoroughly believe that no power in the universe can withhold from anyone anything they really deserve."

~

- "The whole point is to discipline the mind."

~

- "All differences in this world are of degree, and not of kind because oneness is the secret of everything."

~

- "If you have infinite patience and perseverance, success is bound to come. No mistake in that."

~

- "Do not lower your goals to the level of your abilities. Instead, raise your abilities to the height of your goals."

XXIX
Famous Quotes

Positive Attitude Quotes for a Positive Life

"If you have a positive attitude and constantly strive to give your best effort, eventually you will overcome your immediate problems and find you are ready for greater challenges."
- *Pat Riley*

~

"A positive attitude is something everyone can work on, and everyone can learn how to employ it."
- *Joan Lunden*

~

"A positive attitude causes a chain reaction of positive thoughts, events and outcomes. It is a catalyst and it sparks extraordinary results."
- *Wade Boggs*

~

"I think that life is difficult. People have challenges. Family members get sick, people get older, you don't always get the job or the promotion that you want. You have conflicts in your life. And really, life is about your resilience and your ability to go through your life and all of the ups and downs with a positive attitude."
- *Jennifer Hyman*

~

"Believe it first - If you can think it, then you can do it.."
– *Partha Goswami*

~

"You just keep a positive attitude no matter what comes in your way - challenges, roadblocks - don't let it faze you, and you can overcome anything."
- *Rose Namajunas*

~

"Adopting a really positive attitude can work wonders to adding years to your life, a spring to your step, a sparkle to your eye, and all of that."
- *Christie Brinkley*

~

"A positive attitude is not going to save you. What it's going to do is, every day, between now and the day you die, whether that's a short time from now or a long time from now, that every day, you're going to actually live."
- *Elizabeth Edwards*

~

"Chaotic people often have chaotic lives, and I think they create that. But if you try to have inner peace and a positive attitude, I think you attract that."
- *Imelda Staunton*

~

"Natural ability is important, but you can go far without it if you have the focus, drive, desire and positive attitude."
- *Kirsten Sweetland*

~

"Know that your success is based entirely on your attitude, your commitment, and your self-discipline. You are the only person who can generate a new mindset."
- *Ellen Mensap*

~

"Learning to control and adjust your attitude to a positive one reflects the wisdom of the mind."
- *Catherine Pulsifer*

~

"A positive attitude is a person's passport to a better tomorrow."
- *Jeff Keller*

~

"Attitude is a way of life. We have a choice every day regarding the attitude we embrace for that day."

- Puneet Sharma

~

"Think big, think fast, think ahead. Ideas are no one's monopoly."
- Dhirubhai Ambani

~

"The place to start a positive attitude is with the little things. If you can learn to appreciate them and be grateful for them, you'll appreciate the big things as well as everything in between."
- John Maxwell

~

"Positive anything is better than negative nothing."
- Elbert Hubbard

~

"All our dreams can come true if we have the courage to pursue them."
– Walt Disney

~

"The secret of getting ahead is getting started."
– Mark Twain

~

"I've missed more than 9,000 shots in my career. I've lost almost 300 games. 26 times I've been trusted to take the game-winning shot and missed. I've failed over and over and over again in my life and that is why I succeed."
– Michael Jordan

~

"When one door of happiness closes, another opens; but often we look so long at the closed door that we do not see the one which has been opened for us."
— Helen Keller

~

"Whatever you are, be a good one."
— Abraham Lincoln

~

"With the realization of one's own potential and self-confidence in one's ability, one can build a better world."
— Dalai Lama

~

"Spread love everywhere you go. Let no one ever come to you without leaving happier."

— Mother Teresa

~

"Success is not final; failure is not fatal: It is the courage to continue that counts."

— Winston S. Churchill

~

"A day without laughter is a day wasted."

– Charlie Chaplin

~

"Your imagination is your preview of life's coming attractions."

– Albert Einstein

~

"All of us do not have equal talent. But, all of us have an equal opportunity to develop our talents."

– Dr. A P J Abdul Kalam

~

"If I can't make it through one door, I'll go through another door- or i'll make a door. Something terrific will come no matter how dark the present."

— Rabindranath Tagore

~

"If you want to walk fast, walk alone. But if you want to walk far, walk together"

— Ratan Tata

~

"If you don't build your dream, someone else will hire you to help them build theirs."

— Dhirubhai Ambani

~

"With a positive attitude, it is possible to turn situations of failure into success."

- Dan Miller

~

"Change is the nature of life but challenge is the future of life. So challenge the changes. Never change the challenges."

- Amitabh Bachchan

~

"Motivation is like fire—unless you keep adding fuel to it, it dies. Your fuel is your belief in your inner values."

- Shiv Khera

~

"Whatever you do, do it with a passion or else don't."
- Sandeep Maheshwari

~

"You must begin to think of yourself as becoming the person you want to be."
- Vivek Vindra

How To Start

I Can.....

"Believe it first - If you can think it, then you can do it.."
– Partha Goswami

XXX

Using Positive Affirmations

How To Start Using Positive Affirmations

1. Speak and Repeat Positive Affirmations Out Loud

Speaking reinforces our learning and increases the likelihood of our subconscious actually hearing our request. By creating a habit like this that is repeated consistently and linked with the affirmations, you are building neural connections that can make the affirmation stronger.

2. Use the Present Tense When Saying Positive Affirmations

Concepts like "soon" or "later" or "better" lack clarity and can allow your affirmation to lose focus and efficacy. By being clear and indicating in the phrase that we already are or have what we desire, we start generating the emotions that come from the statement actually being true.

3. Avoid negatives in positive affirmations

Be careful not to use negatives in your affirmations. Choose your message carefully to ensure your words speak to the positive present and future you want to create.

4. Create positive affirmations that are meaningful to you

Some generic affirmations like "I am confident" or "I am happy" can feel a bit inauthentic, generating some friction between the words and your current feelings about yourself. If you're feeling this way, try generating affirmations that feel *true to you*. Perhaps, "I am capable of manifesting my dreams", or "I am someone who can accept love into my life". Affirmations can be very individual and their success may in part depend on how these words resonate with you as a unique individual.

5. Craft positive affirmations that are specific, simple, and direct

Your conscious mind knows what it wants but it needs agreement from your unconscious mind.Once you have a detailed positive affirmation that you feel good about, try it out and see how it makes you feel. If it doesn't make you feel better, rework your affirmation until it does.

6. Fill your positive affirmations with passion

Positive affirmations that are full of emotion and genuine belief have a greater impact. By filling your affirmations with positive emotions, they can be much more effective in bringing about what you desire.

7. Add visualizations to your positive affirmations

Use your conscious mind to design a scene that supports your positive affirmations. The clearer you can see what you are dreaming of manifesting, the better your affirmation can support it.

8. Ground your positive affirmations in your body

Use facial expressions, gung-ho gestures, thumbs-up, affirmative sounds like "Whoah!" or "Yes I can!", clap your hands, or jump up and down. Another way to get your message into your body is to exercise or take walk while repeating your affirmations. The mental-somatic connections in the brain are thus reinforced and can provide greater support to your positive affirmation.

9. Take action on your positive affirmations

Ground your positive affirmations in reality by taking some action. If it's a job you are looking for, send out some resumes. Actions speak even louder than words.

10. Stick to your positive affirmations

It takes time to reprogram your brain. Remind yourself to do your positive affirmations by putting up sticky note reminders around your home, or paint a rock as a trigger-reminder, or change your cellphone lock screen. Every time you see it or just think of your object, state out loud your positive affirmation.

Yes...I Can

~

Cryptoxic

~

A Brief on Bloc

~

Be Positive

~

The Goal

~

Others